ULTIMATE GUIDE TO THE
PREMIER LEAGUE 2020

WRITTEN BY ROB MASON

PICTURE RESEARCH BY CAMERON PRENTICE

DESIGNED BY LUCY BOYD

PBR

A Pillar Box Red Publication

© 2019. Published by Pillar Box Red Publishing Limited, in association with the Daily Mirror. Printed in the EU.

This is an independent publication. It has no connection with the Premier League, the clubs featured, individuals featured or with any organisation or individual connected in any way whatsoever with the Premier League, the clubs, organisations or individuals featured.

Any quotes within this publication which are attributed to anyone connected to the Premier League, the clubs, organisations or individuals have been sourced from other publications, or from the internet and, as such, are a matter of public record.

Whilst every effort has been made to ensure the accuracy of information within this publication, the publisher shall have no liability to any person or entity with respect to any inaccuracy, misleading information, loss or damage caused directly or indirectly by the information contained within this book.

The views expressed are solely those of the author and do not reflect the opinions of Pillar Box Red Publishing Limited. All rights reserved.

ISBN: 978-1-912456-36-9

Images © PA Images.

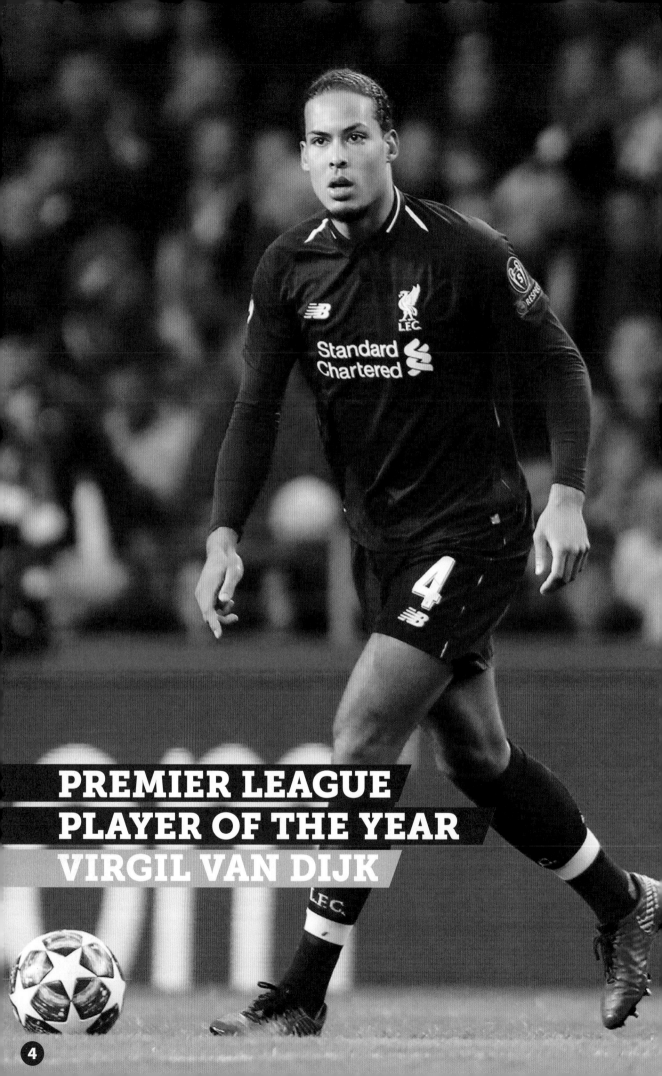

PREMIER LEAGUE PLAYER OF THE YEAR
VIRGIL VAN DIJK

CONTENTS

QUICK OFF THE MARK

Southampton striker Shane Long scored the fastest ever goal in the Premier League.

He scored just 7.69 seconds into the game when Watford visited St. Mary's in April. What was just as amazing is that Watford kicked off!

The ball was played back to Hornets defender Craig Cathcart but Long charged down his clearance, raced onto the loose ball and cleverly chipped the ball over Watford 'keeper Ben Foster.

QUICKEST PREMIER LEAGUE GOALS

07.69 seconds Shane Long for Southampton at Watford	2018/19
09.82 seconds Ledley King for Spurs at Bradford City	2000/01
10.52 seconds Alan Shearer for Newcastle at home to Man City	2002/03
10.54 seconds Christian Eriksen for Spurs at home to Man United	2017/18
11.90 seconds Mark Viduka for Leeds at Charlton	2001/02

PREMIER PREDICTIONS

The Premier League table at Christmas is not going to be in the same order come the end of the season after the final games are played on 17 May.

Will the team who top the table as Santa arrives be the team still on top when the Premier League winners are decided? Will the bottom three at Christmas be the three who go down? If not, who are the team most likely to slide into the Championship having been outside the bottom three in late December?

Your challenge is to use your skill and knowledge to see how accurately you can predict where teams will end up when it comes to crunch time of the campaign. Sometime before New Year's Day write down which position you think each club will end up in and, when the season is over, take a look at your own predictions and see how well you can predict the outcome of the league!

	MY PREDICTION	ACTUAL PLACE
ARSENAL		
ASTON VILLA		
BOURNEMOUTH		
BRIGHTON & HOVE ALBION		
BURNLEY		
CHELSEA		
CRYSTAL PALACE		
EVERTON		
LEICESTER CITY		
LIVERPOOL		
MANCHESTER CITY		
MANCHESTER UNITED		
NEWCASTLE UNITED		
NORWICH CITY		
SHEFFIELD UNITED		
SOUTHAMPTON		
TOTTENHAM HOTSPUR		
WATFORD		
WEST HAM UNITED		
WOLVERHAMPTON WANDERERS		

SECOND HALF OF THE SEASON

In the Premier League every game counts, right from the season opener when Liverpool hosted Norwich on 9 August to the final day of the campaign on Sunday 17 May.

While you get the same number of points for beating an opponent in April as you do in August there can be no doubt that the nearer you get to the end of the season the more vital every point can be. Take a look at these key fixtures for the second half of the season. Every one of them is set to be a really important match and one to keep your eye on.

Please note that the dates of all of the matches (except the final day fixtures) may move slightly if they are chosen to be live TV games.

BOXING DAY

LEICESTER CITY v LIVERPOOL

Liverpool have edged their last two Premier League visits to the Kingpower Stadium but Leicester won the two before that, both by a two goal margin. Under former Liverpool and Celtic manager Brendan Rodgers, Leicester are a well organised and talented team capable of giving even Liverpool a tough time. This will be the fifth time the Foxes have met the Reds on Boxing Day. Liverpool have won twice, Leicester once and there has been one draw.

MY SCORE PREDICTION	ACTUAL SCORE

NEW YEAR'S DAY

ARSENAL v MANCHESTER UNITED

These two missed out on the top four last season and neither will want to do so again, so this could be a brilliant game to start 2020 with. Games between the Gunners and the Red Devils have a history of being tasty and that makes this fixture all the more eagerly awaited. Last season Arsenal won 2-0 at the Emirates but Manchester United also won by two clear goals there in the FA Cup, just as they had in the Premier League the previous season. Can they spoil the Gunners start to the new year?

MY SCORE PREDICTION	ACTUAL SCORE

TITLE SHOWDOWN

4th APRIL 2020
MANCHESTER CITY v LIVERPOOL

It is only two seasons since City beat Liverpool 5-0 in this fixture but surely no one could imagine them managing such a big win again. Last season just a point separated the teams at the end of the season. Will it be as close this time? The winners of this game will give themselves a massive boost with just a handful of fixtures to play after this one.

MY SCORE PREDICTION	ACTUAL SCORE

TOUGH RUN IN

9th MAY 2020
LIVERPOOL v CHELSEA

If Liverpool are going to stop Manchester City retaining their title the Reds are going to have to do it the hard way. Two of their last three games are away to Arsenal and this final home fixture against Chelsea will be a repeat of the start of season European Super Cup meeting between the winners of the Champions League and the Europa League. It could well be a game both top teams are desperate to win – but only one can and which one will it be?

MY SCORE PREDICTION	ACTUAL SCORE

FINAL DAY FIXTURES

Will the race for the Premier League title be settled before the final day or, like last season, will it go down to the wire? Possible contenders Spurs and Liverpool face tricky final day fixtures at Crystal Palace and Newcastle, while favourites Manchester City host Norwich who will be hoping to be safe by then following their promotion last season.

What about the race for the Champions League places, and who will be battling to stay in the Premier League? The final day of the season always has some issues to resolve which makes it such an exciting day. As fans prepare for a summer without the Premier League it reminds us of what we'll be missing until it all gets going again in August when the 2020/21 season starts!

17th MAY 2020	MY SCORE PREDICTION	ACTUAL SCORE
ARSENAL v WATFORD		
BURNLEY v BRIGHTON & HOVE ALBION		
CHELSEA v WOLVERHAMPTON WANDERERS		
CRYSTAL PALACE v TOTTENHAM HOTSPUR		
EVERTON v BOURNEMOUTH		
LEICESTER CITY v MANCHESTER UNITED		
NEWCASTLE UNITED v LIVERPOOL		
MANCHESTER CITY v NORWICH CITY		
SOUTHAMPTON v SHEFFIELD UNITED		
WEST HAM UNITED v ASTON VILLA		

GOALS OF THE SEASON

There were some great goals scored in the Premier League in 2018/19 with Andros Townsend of Crystal Palace scoring the best of them. Townsend's fabulous volley helped to inflict champions Manchester City's only home defeat of the season. It needed something that special to beat them!

DISTANCE: 30.6 yards

SPEED: 78.2mph

"Everything about the goal, the opponent, the strike, it was perfection. I think it was a strike like that needed to beat the champions away from home. I'm thankful it kind of dropped nicely to my left foot. I hit it clean and the rest is history...I still don't know how I managed to hit it that perfectly from that far out."

Andros Townsend

GOAL OF THE SEASON SHORT LIST

These top 10 goals were short-listed for the Goal of the Season:

1. Jean Michaël Seri – **Fulham** v Burnley
2. Daniel Sturridge – Chelsea v **Liverpool**
3. Aaron Ramsey – Fulham v **Arsenal**
4. Son Heung-min – **Tottenham Hotspur** v Chelsea
5. Andros Townsend – Manchester City v **Crystal Palace**
6. André Schürrle – Burnley v **Fulham**
7. Fabian Schär – **Newcastle** v Burnley
8. Anthony Knockaert – Crystal Palace v **Brighton & Hove Albion**
9. Eden Hazard – **Chelsea** v West Ham
10. Vincent Kompany – **Manchester City** v Leicester City

- Only relegated Fulham had more than one goal nominated – Seri's strike v Burnley and Schürrle's volley at Burnley.

- None of the Premier League's joint Golden Boot winners (Pierre-Emerick Aubameyang, Mo Salah or Sadio Mané) had a goal on the shortlist.

- Match of the Day made Vincent Kompany's great shot against Leicester for Man City their goal of the season – but only after their panel overcame the public vote which counted for 10%. The majority of the public voted for Townsend's terrific shot.

- Townsend's goal helped Palace win 3-2. It was the BBC's Goal of the Month for December and Palace's Goal of the Season as well as the Premier League's Goal of the Season.

PIERRE-EMERICK AUBAMEYANG

22 PREMIER LEAGUE GOALS 2018/19

2 MOST GOALS SCORED IN A PREMIER LEAGUE GAME

17 PREMIER LEAGUE GAMES SCORED IN

31 TOTAL GOALS SCORED IN 2018/19

3 MOST GOALS SCORED IN ANY GAME (v Valencia, Europa League)

CLUB: **Arsenal**

INTERNATIONAL TEAM: **Gabon**

DID YOU KNOW:

Having signed from Borussia Dortmund in January 2018 he scored his first 25 Premier League goals for Arsenal in just 37 games? That's quicker than Thierry Henry (42 games) and Ian Wright (51 games).

SADIO MANÉ

22 PREMIER LEAGUE
GOALS 2018/19

2 MOST GOALS SCORED
IN A PREMIER LEAGUE GAME

16 PREMIER LEAGUE GAMES
SCORED IN

27 TOTAL GOALS SCORED
IN 2018/19

2 MOST GOALS SCORED IN
ANY GAME

CLUB: **Liverpool**

INTERNATIONAL TEAM: **Senegal**

DID YOU KNOW:

Mané scored the quickest ever Premier
League hat-trick, taking just two minutes
56 seconds to score three times for
Southampton against Villa in 2015.

MO SALAH

22 PREMIER LEAGUE GOALS 2018/19

3 MOST GOALS SCORED IN A PREMIER LEAGUE GAME (v Bournemouth)

18 PREMIER LEAGUE GAMES SCORED IN

29 TOTAL GOALS SCORED IN 2018/19

3 MOST GOALS SCORED IN ANY GAME

CLUB: **Liverpool**

INTERNATIONAL TEAM: **Egypt**

DID YOU KNOW:

Mo Salah first played at Anfield in 2014 for Chelsea!

ALISSON

221 PREMIER LEAGUE
CLEAN SHEETS 2018/19

3 MOST PREMIER LEAGUE GAMES
IN A ROW WITHOUT CONCEDING

5 MOST GAMES IN A ROW IN ALL
COMPETITIONS WITHOUT CONCEDING

3 MOST GOALS CONCEDED
IN A PREMIER LEAGUE GAME
(Liverpool 4-3 Crystal Palace)

CLUB: **Liverpool**

INTERNATIONAL TEAM: **Brazil**

DID YOU KNOW:

Alisson's older brother Muriel is a goalkeeper who plays in Portugal.

RACE FOR THE TITLE

Manchester City had to be relentlessly consistent to pip Liverpool to the Premier League by a point. No team had ever had as many as Liverpool's 97 points and not won the title. The Reds' total would have been enough to win the Premier League in every season except the last two. Jürgen Klopp's men set a new record for the number of points needed to be runners-up in any of Europe's top five leagues. The previous record was Real Madrid's 96 in 2009/10. Like Liverpool, they too missed out by one point and, like Liverpool, they lost out to Pep Guardiola who was then the manager of Barcelona! So how did City do it?

7 OCTOBER

LIVERPOOL 0-0 MAN CITY
MAHREZ MISS

With Sergio Aguero already subbed, Riyad Mahrez stepped up to take a late penalty – and blasted it over the bar! The points were shared with City, Liverpool and Chelsea all level on 20 points from eight games, with City top on goal difference.

29 DECEMBER

LIVERPOOL 5-1 ARSENAL
REDS NINE POINTS CLEAR

Klopp's Reds strode nine points clear of second placed Spurs with a Roberto Firmino hat-trick destroying Arsenal as Liverpool won a ninth successive Premier League fixture. City were a point and a place behind Spurs but with a game in hand. It hadn't been a happy Christmas for City who lost twice in four days either side of Christmas, the first at home to Palace, when Andros Townsend scorched home the goal of the season.

3 JANUARY

MAN CITY 2-1 LIVERPOOL
TURNING POINT

The title race was re-ignited as Leroy Sané scored the goal that brought Liverpool's only defeat of the season. The Anfield club's lead was cut to four points, terrible given that, had they won, they would have opened up a double-digit lead on City. Before Aguero gave City the lead, Liverpool had gone within 1.12cm of scoring! John Stones managed to clear in the nick of time after Sadio Mané hit the post and Stones' attempted clearance looked like going in but hit his own 'keeper Ederson! Had Liverpool taken the lead they might have maintained that gap over City – a gap that it took City 14 wins in a row to wipe out!

"We knew it was a final today, if we lose it is almost over."

PEP GUARDIOLA

17

23 FEBRUARY

BURNLEY 2-1 TOTTENHAM HOTSPUR
SPURS DROP OUT

Tottenham's challenge was a real one. Reaching the Champions League final and knocking Man City out along the way showed they were serious. The sight of Mauricio Pochettino uncharacteristically confronting referee Mike Dean at the final whistle showed that Spurs knew the game was up. A late goal from Ashley Barnes left the Londoners five points behind City and Liverpool – with Liverpool still having the advantage of a game in hand.

3 MARCH

EVERTON 0-0 LIVERPOOL
DROPPED POINTS

Jordan Pickford's clean sheet in the Merseyside derby meant the last points dropped by either Liverpool or City in the title race. The dropped two points were the seventh and eighth points the Reds had failed to collect in a stuttering six game run. That sequence started with Leicester holding Liverpool at Anfield at the end of January and included draws at West Ham and Man United. Liverpool won their remaining nine games after their draw at Goodison Park but the damage had been done.

20 APRIL

MAN CITY 1-0 TOTTENHAM HOTSPUR
SPURS CAN'T STOP CITY

Phil Foden's early diving header put City back to the top of the Premier League table. The result left City one point better off than Liverpool with each having eight games to play. Liverpool had seen Spurs' visit to the Etihad as a chance of City dropping points and they did need Ederson to make a string of important saves, especially from Son Heung-min. By now Spurs were 19 points off top spot – their challenge long since over.

24 APRIL

MAN UTD 0-2 MAN CITY
NO DERBY DRAMA

It's not often that Liverpool supporters like to see Manchester United win but Reds fans were united in wanting to see a home win at Old Trafford. For City it was just another test to pass – which they did with second half goals from Bernardo Silva and Leroy Sané. The result kept that single point advantage for City over Liverpool, with games running out.

TABLE TOPPERS

Liverpool topped the table for 141 days – 16 more than City but it is who tops it after 38 games that counts. Chelsea topped the table for nine days. City were the first team to retain the title in 11 years but Liverpool had the consolation of going on to win the Champions League!

4 MAY

NEWCASTLE UNITED 2-3 LIVERPOOL
REDS KEEP GOING

Squashed in between Liverpool's two legs of their Champions League semi-final with Barcelona, this could have been the game where they slipped up. Newcastle had sensationally beaten Manchester City earlier in the season and, having twice fought back after Liverpool took the lead, Rafa Benitez's side looked capable of effectively handing the title to City. However, Liverpool had everything you could want from champions – except for the Premier League trophy in the final analysis. For all of their much-vaunted front three of Salah (who scored here), Sané and Firmino, it was Divock Origi who scored some of their most important goals of the season including the late winner here. The result left Liverpool two points better off than City, keeping the pressure on the Mancunians who had two games left to play compared to Liverpool's one.

6 MAY

MAN CITY 1-0 LEICESTER CITY
STARRY, STARRY NIGHT

Liverpool's victory at Newcastle meant that City had to beat 2016 champions Leicester – now revitalised under new boss and ex-Liverpool supremo Brendan Rodgers and with the son of Manchester United legend Schmeichel in goal (this time it being Kasper not Peter).

The Foxes were tough opponents. Well organised and determined, they stifled such a lot of City's free-flowing football. Unusually, City struggled to find space and, as the clock started to tick down, thoughts were just starting to surface that perhaps, just perhaps, the title balance would switch to Liverpool. City needed something special and they of all teams possessed an array of special players who could conjure up something magical when it was needed: Agüero, B. Silva, D. Silva, Sané, Mahrez, De Bruyne, Foden, it was a long list but then Vincent Kompany strode forward with the ball. With plenty of options ahead of Kompany, Pep Guardiola was saying 'No shoot Vinnie, no shoot!' as his captain shaped to fire goal-wards from 25 yards. It would be Kompany's final home game as he left for Anderlecht at the end of the season. Famed for stopping goals rather than scoring them Vincent chose this starry, starry night to score the goal that defined the title race – incredibly special.

MAY 12

BRIGHTON 1-4 MAN CITY
TO THE WIRE

City winning at Brighton to seal the title on the final day seemed a formality but when Glenn Murray put the Seagulls ahead mid-way through the first half hearts fluttered at Anfield, where Liverpool had to defeat Wolves, and hope. Stung, City equalised within a minute through Agüero and led before half-time via Laporte. Second half goals from Mahrez and Gundogan saw City home in a canter, Liverpool's 2-0 beating of Wolves rendered matter-less.

32 CHANGES

During the title race the team at the top of the table changed an incredible 32 times! This was often due to staggered kick off times but is still an incredible statistic that set a new Premier League record. The previous highest number of table-topping changes was in 2001/02 when the leadership between Arsenal and Manchester United changed on 28 occasions.

It was the ninth time the Premier League title had been decided on the final day of the season. Just one point behind City, Liverpool were an astonishing 25 points ahead of third placed Chelsea. To look 25 points beneath Chelsea would take you into the bottom half of the table, two points behind 12th placed Palace who finished on 49.

Pressure from an excellent Liverpool had forced City into relentlessly having to win their last 14 games in order to edge the title. A season earlier Liverpool had been 25 points behind City and in 2019/20 will look to become Premier League champions for the first time.

MOST POINTS FOR TOP TWO

New record set in each of the last three seasons

2016/17	179 points Chelsea & Spurs
2017/18	181 points Man City & Man Utd
2018/19	195 points Man City & Liverpool

PREMIER LEAGUE TEAM OF THE SEASON

ANDREW ROBERTSON
Left back – Liverpool

Scotland full back Robertson is an outstanding defender – and just as good going forward. No wonder Liverpool score so many when they have brilliance from the wings with quality from both sides.

VIRGIL VAN DIJK
Central defender – Liverpool

The top defender in the Premier League and probably the world. Liverpool had a problem with their defence and solved it with the signing of Van Dijk.

EDERSON MORAES
Goalkeeper – Man City

When you are in goal for Man City you aren't often needed but your concentration has to be spot on. Ederson's is and he's great with his feet too.

AYMERIC LAPORTE
Central defender – Man City

Man City's team is full of attacking talent. French defender Laporte gives them some balance and especially now Vincent Kompany has gone he is even more important.

TRENT ALEXANDER-ARNOLD
Right back – Liverpool

The young Liverpool and England full back is a fantastic assist maker. He's super-fast on the flanks and delivers top quality crosses.

Every season the players themselves vote for their team of the season. This is the Professional Footballers' Association Team Of The Year.

PAUL POGBA

Midfielder – Man Utd

The World Cup winner was the only player in the PFA team who didn't play for one of the top two teams. Pogba's power, his box to box dominance and his quality under pressure make him a word star.

RAHEEM STERLING

Forward – Man City

Has gone from good player to great player. Always lightning quick, Sterling's end product has improved as he's got older and wiser.

FERNANDINHO

Midfielder – Man City

The Brazilian keeps City ticking. He sees everything and dictates the pace of the game. If teams break at his defence he is the first to spot the danger as well as being at the base of their attacks.

SERGIO AGÜERO

Forward – Man City

Year in, year out Agüero delivers: 21 Premier goals and 32 altogether in 2018/19 – including three hat-tricks!

BERNARDO SILVA

Midfielder – Man City

Bernardo Silva's work rate matches his fantastic quality, making him so vital for City that no forward played more as City won the Premier League.

SADIO MANÉ

Forward – Liverpool

Fast and fabulous, Mané was the 2018/19 joint top Premier League scorer with 22 goals – and 27 in total.

REPORT CARD

Give your grade to each of the teams to play in the Premier League in 2019, based on how well you think they did. Mark them from A+ to F-. If, for instance, you think Manchester City were A+ then write that grade inside the box next to their name. If you think relegated Fulham were F-, especially given all the money they spent only to go straight back down, then put F- in their box.

	Team	Notes	Your Grade
1	**MANCHESTER CITY**	Premier League Champions. FA Cup Winners. Carabao Cup Winners	
2	**LIVERPOOL**	Premier League runners-up. Champions League Winners	
3	**CHELSEA**	Europa League Winners. Carabao Cup finalists	
4	**SPURS**	Champions League finalists. Carabao Cup semi-finalists	
5	**ARSENAL**	Europa League finalists	
6	**MAN UNITED**	Europa League qualification. Replaced Jose Mourinho with Ole Gunnar Solskjaer.	
7	**WOLVES**	Europa League qualification. FA Cup semi-finalists	
8	**EVERTON**	Finished three points and one place away from European qualification and made early exits from both cups.	
9	**LEICESTER CITY**	Lost on penalties to Man City in Carabao Cup quarter final. Replaced Claude Puel with Brendan Rodgers	
10	**WEST HAM UNITED**	Humbled in the FA Cup, losing 4-2 at AFC Wimbledon.	
11	**WATFORD**	FA Cup finalists	
12	**CRYSTAL PALACE**	Only team to beat Man City on their own ground.	

	Team	Notes	Your Grade
13	**NEWCASTLE UNITED**	Last team to beat Man City	
14	**BOURNEMOUTH**	Beat Chelsea 4-0 but conceded more goals than anyone outside the relegation zone.	
15	**BURNLEY**	Only 12 points from first half of the season but a big improvement after that.	
16	**SOUTHAMPTON**	Improved after appointing Ralph Hasenhuttl	
17	**BRIGHTON & HOVE ALBION**	FA Cup semi-finalists. Sacked Chris Hughton at the end of the season.	
18	**CARDIFF CITY**	Unlucky to go down after scrapping hard all season. Had some big decisions go against them and suffered the tragic loss of striker Emiliano Sala being killed in an air crash when they hoped he would score the goals to keep them up.	
19	**FULHAM**	Spent £100m after being promoted then sacked Slavisa Jokanovic. Appointed Claudio Ranieri who lasted just 106 days before being replaced by Scott Parker.	
20	**HUDDERSFIELD TOWN**	Finished bottom in their second season in the Premier League.	
1	**NORWICH CITY**	Promoted as Champions	
	SHEFFIELD UNITED	Won automatic promotion two seasons after coming up from League One.	
	ASTON VILLA	Won promotion via the Play-offs after scintillating form in the second half of the season under Dean Smith.	

CHRISTMAS CRACKERS

Christmas Cracker games with crazy score-lines, together with hat-tricks and a (Christmas) red card or two thrown in for good measure, make Christmas time in the Premier League a time to celebrate. Maybe there'll be a Christmas cracker of a game this year...

Boxing Day 2012
MANCHESTER UTD 4-3 NEWCASTLE UTD

This was Sir Alex Ferguson's final Boxing Day fixture and his team clinched the points in 'Fergie-time' with an added time winner from Javier Hernández after coming from behind three times!

Boxing Day 2007
CHELSEA 4-4 ASTON VILLA

Three red cards and eight goals, including a last minute equaliser from the penalty spot! Two goals from Andriy Shevchenko brought Avram Grant's Chelsea level after Shaun Maloney had put Villa two up. It was then Villa's turn to equalise through Martin Lauren after Alex put the Blues ahead, but when a Michael Ballack free-kick made it 4-3 to Chelsea late on it looked all over, until a last minute penalty from Gareth Barry made it four all as Ashley Cole was sent off for conceding the penalty – joining Ricardo Carvalho and Villa's Zat Knight in having an early bath.

29 December 2007
SPURS 6-4 READING

Dimitar Berbatov ruined Reading's Christmas with four goals as the away side handed him some late Christmas presents.

29 December 2012
ARSENAL 7-3 NEWCASTLE UTD

Eight goals in the second half included Arsenal scoring four in the final 17 minutes as Theo Walcott claimed a hat-trick.

Boxing Day 2017
SPURS 5-2 SOUTHAMPTON

Harry Kane broke Alan Shearer's record for goals in a calendar year, finishing with 39 from 36 games after a hat-trick against the Saints.

DENYING THE DROP

Brighton & Hove Albion, Southampton and Burnley all had relegation worries last season but survived them. They'll all want to be a lot higher this season. Let's take a look at their vital stats and chances this season...

BRIGHTON & HOVE ALBION

2019 Position:	17th
Points Clear of Relegation:	2
Top Premier League Scorer:	13 Glenn Murray
Player of the Year:	Shane Duffy

Having replaced manager Chris Hughton with Graham Potter, the Seagulls are hoping to improve but with their main goal-scorer Glenn Murray turning 36 a month into this season, Albion have to find goals or face danger. Big money signings Alireza Jahanbakhsh and Yves Bissouma failed to make an impact in their first year and the south coast club can't keep relying on old stagers. Lewis Dunk, Shane Duffy, Maty Ryan and Murray need some help!

Test Yourself:
1. Which trophy was presented at Albion's Amex Stadium in 2019?

....

SOUTHAMPTON

2019 Position:	16th
Points Clear of Relegation:	5
Top Premier League Scorer:	7 Danny Ings & James Ward Prowse
Player of the Year:	Nathan Redmond

A bad start to the season saw Mark Hughes sacked just before Christmas after taking just nine points from 14 games. Replacement Ralph Hasenhüttl became the first Austrian manager in the Premier League, steering the Saints to safety with two games to spare. Under Hasenhüttl, Southampton managed 30 points from 23 matches and will expect to finish much higher this season.

Test Yourself:

2. As an international player was Ralph Hasenhüttl a centre-back or a centre-forward?

....

BURNLEY

2019 Position:	15th
Points Clear of Relegation:	6
Top Premier League Scorer:	12 Ashley Barnes
Player of the Year:	Ashley Westwood

A bad start to the season came after the Clarets started in the Europa League, but twice managing to win three games in a row kept them safe despite 20 defeats. Having finished seventh a year earlier it was always going to be tough to match that, but the second half of the season showed that the men from Turf Moor are a solid and well organised side more than capable of holding their own in the Premier League.

Test Yourself:

3. Burnley have three England goalkeepers; Joe Hart, Nick Pope and who else?

....

Test yourself answers on page 61

KINGS

OF EUROPE

The Premier League's place as the world's top league was clearly shown in 2019 when both European finals were all Premier League affairs.

Liverpool beat Tottenham in the Champions League final in Madrid while Chelsea saw off Arsenal almost 3,000 miles from London in Baku, the capital of Azerbaijan – leaving Liverpool and Chelsea to face each other in the European Super Cup in Istanbul. Liverpool won that trophy too, having beaten the Blues on penalties after an exciting 2-2 draw.

All this and the Premier League champions Manchester City weren't involved – they were knocked out of the Champions League by Spurs.

The Champions League semi-finals had held all the drama – Liverpool somehow beating Barcelona 4-0 at Anfield having lost the first leg 3-0. Spurs' achievement in reaching the final was just as sensational. Having already knocked out Man City, Tottenham

lost their first leg semi-final at home to a vibrant young Ajax team. However, Spurs went to Amsterdam and found a way to win, despite being 3-0 down on aggregate ten minutes into the second half.

Step forward Lucas Moura. Two goals in four minutes from the Brazilian brought Tottenham back into it but the game looked up as it ticked into the sixth minute of added time. With just a few seconds to play Moura completed his hat-trick and through the away goals rule Spurs went from vanquished to victors in the blink of an eye.

A second minute Mo Salah penalty in the final gave Liverpool momentum in Madrid. This time Tottenham couldn't respond and when Divock Origi – one of the heroes of the semi-final – added a late second the Champions League Trophy was heading to Anfield for the sixth time.

Four days earlier a five goal second half had entertained the continent as Chelsea took the Europa League, defeating Arsenal 4-1. Olivier Giroud, Pedro and Eden Hazard put Chelsea three up with Hazard quickly adding another after the goal of the game from Alex Iwobi threatened to bring the Gunners back into it.

VIRGIL VAN DIJK

In a game full of world class strikers there seem to be far fewer world class defenders but there is no doubt that Liverpool centre-back Virgil Van Dijk is totally brilliant.

The Premier League Player of the Season for 2018/19, the Netherlands international is used to gaining individual as well as team awards.

Liverpool's current Player of the Season, Virgil also won Player of the Year awards when he was at Southampton and Celtic as well as a long list of individual awards and Team of the Year selections. Twice a Scottish Premier League winner with Celtic, Van Dijk now wants an English Premier League medal to go with his Champions League winner's medal.

Currently at the peak of his career, Virgil is captain of his country and cost Liverpool a world record fee for a defender when they paid £75m to Southampton in January 2018. Given how much he has improved the Reds defence that fee is looking a bargain now!

TEN THINGS TO KNOW ABOUT VIRGIL

1. Height: 1.93m
2. Age: 27 (Born 8 July 1991)
3. Played for Groningen, Celtic, Southampton and Liverpool.
4. Made his debut for Groningen v ADO Den Haag in May 2011.
5. Was a teammate of Norwich star Teemu Pukki at Celtic, on one occasion both of them scoring twice in a Champions League match.
6. Signed for Dutch legend Ronald Koeman at Southampton, costing the Saints £13m in 2015.
7. Was later made captain of his country by Ronald Koeman.
8. Moved on to Liverpool for £75m in January 2018.
9. Became the first player since 1901 to debut with a goal in the Merseyside derby.
10. Was UEFA's Man of the Match in the 2019 Champions League final.

CHERRY BLOSSOM

AFC Bournemouth's Ryan Fraser and Callum Wilson have set a new Premier League record as the most dangerous of dynamic duos.

When Wilson scored from a Fraser assist to earn the Cherries a point in a 3-3 draw with Southampton in April it was the 12th time the pair had combined to produce a Premier League goal during the season.

The strike set a new high in a 38 game Premier League campaign, breaking the record of 11 set by Alan Shearer and Mike Newell for Blackburn in 1995/96.

Fraser created seven goals for Wilson with the England striker returning the favour to the Scotland international five times.

While the AFC Bournemouth duo denied Alan Shearer of one record, the all-time Premier League record scorer still holds the record for the total number of goals scored in combination with a partner overall. In Blackburn's Premier League title winning season of 1994/95 the SAS of Shearer and Sutton combined 13 times in what was then a 42-game season.

DEADLY DUOS
Highest scoring combinations* in the Premier League
*Combinations = where one player scores from an assist by their partner.

DUO	GOALS	GAMES	SEASON
Alan Shearer & Chris Sutton (Blackburn)	13	42	1994/95
Callum Wilson & Ryan Fraser (AFC Bournemouth)	12	38	2018/19
Les Ferdinand & Kevin Gallen (QPR)	11	42	1994/95
Alan Shearer & Mike Newell (Blackburn)	11	38	1995/96
Dennis Bergkamp & Nicholas Anelka (Arsenal)	10	38	1998/99

CHANGING TIMES
IN NORTH LONDON

Spurs have had four successive top four finishes for the first time since 1960-63.

Arsenal have had three consecutive seasons outside the top four of the Premier League for the first time since 1983-86 when they had four seasons out of the top four.

SPURS	PREMIER LEAGUE POSITION	ARSENAL
4th	2018/19	5th
3rd	2017/18	6th
2nd	2016/17	5th
3rd	2015/16	2nd

The changing face of North London football power can be seen as Spurs – now in their brand new stadium – overtake their local rivals Arsenal. The Gunners missed out on the Champions League places for a third year running, just as Tottenham reached the Champions League final while qualifying for the continent's top competition for the fourth year in a row.

Spurs hadn't finished in the top four of the top flight for four years in succession since 1959/60 to 1962/63. Meanwhile Arsenal's Premier League position had seen them qualify for the Champions League for 20 years without fail. In those two decades the Gunners had been Premier League champions three times. Spurs have never won the Premier League and those three Arsenal titles are more than Spurs have won the top league in their entire history.

Is this a long term power change in North London? Can Tottenham keep out-gunning the Gunners or will the red half of North London come back strongly this season and topple Tottenham?

Test Yourself:
1. How many points did Spurs take from their last five Premier League games of 2018/19; 4, 10 or 15?

....

2018/19	PREMIER LEAGUE	FIREPOWER
GOALS SCORED	SPURS 67	ARSENAL 73
GOALS CONCEDED	SPURS 39	ARSENAL 51
POINTS	SPURS 71	ARSENAL 70

Arsenal outscored Spurs by six goals – although Tottenham had to do without Harry Kane for part of the season.

Defensively is where Arsenal lost out – conceding 12 more goals than Spurs. Improving their defence is a must if Arsenal are to get back into the Premier League top four. Only Manchester United in the top nine let in more than Arsenal and even Newcastle who finished 13th conceded three goals fewer than Arsenal.

SPURS TOP PREMIER LEAGUE SCORER	17, Harry Kane
SPURS PLAYER OF THE YEAR	Heung-Min Son
ARSENAL TOP PREMIER LEAGUE SCORER	22, Pierre-Emerick Aubameyang
ARSENAL PLAYER OF THE YEAR	Alexandre Lacazette

FINALISTS

Arsenal reached a European final in 2019, although they were beaten 4-1 by Chelsea in the Europa League. Even that European final appearance by Arsenal was totally overshadowed as Spurs reached the final of the Champions League, a late goal sealing a hard fought defeat to Liverpool.

CUP CLASSICS

When Spurs last finished in the top four for four years in a row they took silverware in three of those years. FA Cup winners in 1961 and 1962 – when they were also league champions – in 1963 Tottenham became the first English club to win a European competition when they lifted the Cup Winners' Cup. In the first of the current run of three seasons when Arsenal have missed out on the top four they at least won the FA Cup.

Test Yourself:
2. Arsenal's best run in last season's Premier League saw them win how many games in row; 5, 6 or 7?
....

Test yourself answers on page 61

CHANGING TIMES IN MANCHESTER

Champions for the last two seasons, City are aiming for a tenth successive year in the top four of the Premier League this season, having been Champions four times in the last nine campaigns. Before this run City had not finished in the top four since 1978.

Sixth last season, United have only finished in the top four twice in the last six years after being Champions five times and runners-up three times in the previous eight campaigns.

CITY	PREMIER LEAGUE POSITION	UNITED
1st	2018/19	6th
1st	2017/18	2nd
3rd	2016/17	6th
4th	2015/16	5th

Last season a gigantic 32 points separated City from United. The Old Trafford team were as close to relegation as they were to champions City, as they had just 32 points more than Cardiff City who went down.

No one has dominated the Premier League as United did. Under Sir Alex Ferguson they were undisputed kings of the competition, winning it in 13 of its first 21 seasons. City in contrast didn't even qualify for Europe through their Premier League placing until 2010, when fifth place took them into the Europa League play-off round.

Now United lag behind their City neighbours. Not only have the Citizens won the Premier League in the last two seasons but they have done so with record points hauls and blitzing record after record as they establish themselves as the top team in the country.

Only Liverpool, and perhaps Spurs, look like they are able to stop City becoming as used to having the Premier League trophy in their trophy cabinet as often as United once

Test Yourself:

1. Huddersfield Town, Southampton and a team who qualified for the Champions League all conceded six goals in a Premier League game with City – name the Champions League side hit for six.

....

38

did. However, United have long been used to being the champions and nothing less than the best will do for their supporters.

United have the ambition and the resources to fight back and try and knock City off their perch as the best team in Manchester and the best in England. Do you think they can do it? Watching United trying to overtake City again is one of the tussles that makes the Premier League so exciting.

conceded more goals (54) than they ever have in the Premier League. So bad were United at the back that at one point they went 13 games without a clean sheet – their worst run since 1971!

2018/19	PREMIER LEAGUE	FIREPOWER
GOALS SCORED	CITY 95	UNITED 65
GOALS CONCEDED	CITY 23	UNITED 54
POINTS	CITY 98	UNITED 66

CITY TOP PREMIER LEAGUE SCORER	21, Sergio Agüero
CITY PLAYER OF THE YEAR	Bernardo Silva
UNITED TOP PREMIER LEAGUE SCORER	13, Paul Pogba
UNITED PLAYER OF THE YEAR	Luke Shaw

City scored almost a third more goals than United and conceded less than half as many. Whereas Arsenal out-scored Spurs but have to improve their defence, United are way behind their Manchester rivals in every department.

At the start of this season United's overall Premier League record showed that they only conceded 0.89 goals per game but in 2018/19 they

CUP CLASSICS

City have won 10 trophies in the last nine seasons – five of them in the last two seasons with 2018/19 bringing the treble of Premier League and both domestic cups. United have not won anything in the last two seasons.

Test Yourself:
2. United's biggest win of last season was 5-1 away to which team who went down but beat them at Old Trafford on the season's final day?

....

Test yourself answers on page 61

NEW GOLD

One of English football's historic clubs Wolverhampton Wanderers returned to the Premier League in 2018/19 and they did so in style! Wolves qualified for Europe by finishing seventh, reached the semi-finals of the FA Cup and achieved the highest position of a newly promoted club since 2001. Famed for their old gold kit, this time the men in old gold performed so well they were the new gold of the Premier League!

HIGHLIGHTS

Achieving a great result against one of the top sides is something most teams in the Premier League are capable of once in a season. In their first year back in the Premier League, Wolves did it 10 times as they achieved their highest league position since 1980 and their first FA Cup semi-final for 21 years.

WOLVES 1-1 MANCHESTER CITY
MANCHESTER UNITED 1-1 WOLVES
ARSENAL 1-1 WOLVES
WOLVES 2-1 CHELSEA
SPURS 1-3 WOLVES
WOLVES 2-1 LIVERPOOL (FA Cup)
CHELSEA 1-1 WOLVES
WOLVES 2-1 MANCHESTER UNITED (FA Cup)
WOLVES 2-1 MANCHESTER UNITED
WOLVES 3-1 ARSENAL

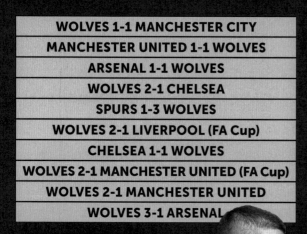

NUNO ESPÍRITO SANTO

Nuno Espírito Santo became head coach of Wolves in May 2017. In his first season he led the club to the Championship title and followed that up with such a great season in the Premier League he was nominated for the Premier League Manager of the Year award.

Unusually for a manager or head coach, Nuno was a goalkeeper in his playing days. He was part of the Portugal squad at the 1996 Olympics and learned from José Mourinho at Porto when they won the Champions League and UEFA Cup.

Becoming a manager himself, Nuno led Portuguese side Rio Ave into Europe for the first time, as well as reaching two cup finals. He then managed Valencia and Porto before coming into English football.

Now regarded as one of the top coaches in the game, his man management is excellent and he requires all of his players to play with high intensity, something that needs supreme fitness. Under Nuno, Wolves' recruitment has been brilliant. They spent over £100m investing in their first season under him in the Premier League. That means Wolves believed in him enough to back him to such an extent financially, but that money needs to be spent

FA CUP

Wolves won at Wembley in 2018/19, but it was against Spurs in the Premier League. They looked like winning at the national stadium again when they led 2-0 against Watford in the FA Cup semi-final only to eventually go down 3-2 after extra-time. The cup run had seen Liverpool, Shrewsbury, Bristol City and Manchester United knocked out, Ruben Neves' brilliant goal being the highlight of the victory over Liverpool.

DID YOU KNOW:

In the home game with Brighton in April Wolves did not commit a single foul. It was the first time any team in the Premier League had done this since 2003/04.

well. Fulham allegedly spent a similar amount of money when promoted alongside Wolves but, unfortunately for them, were immediately relegated. Nuno not only brought in the players he wanted but succeeded in getting them to fit straight in both individually and collectively. Much of what Wolves have achieved so far is without doubt down to him.

PORTUGUESE INFLUENCE

Portuguese manager Nuno Espírito Santo used eight players from Portugal during Wolves first season back in the Premier League. They gave Wolves a fluid style, often playing brilliant eye-catching football that made the men from Molineux one of the most attractive teams in the country. The Portuguese players were: goalkeeper Rui Patrício, young left wing back Rúben Vinagre, midfielders Rúben Neves, Pedro Gonçalves and João Moutinho and forwards Ivan Cavaleiro, Hélder Costa and Diogo Jota.

GOAL OF THE SEASON

Diogo Jota's Goal of the Season against Cardiff at Molineux summed up just how eye-catching Wolves' play was throughout the campaign. The Bluebirds could only sit and watch as Wolves one and two-touch football passed through their midfield and defence. The free-flowing football left the visitors dizzy as just two minutes later Jimenez scored the second in a 2-0 win, this time Jota registering the assist and scoring.

MARVELLOUS MOUTINHO

João Moutinho took the Player of the Season trophy at Wolves end of season awards. The former Sporting, Porto and Monaco midfielder joined Wolves ahead of their return to the Premier League and immediately took English football by storm.

A quality player who won the European Championships in 2016, as well as having a stack of silverware won with his former clubs, João became Wolves Player of the Season after playing in every one of their 38 Premier League fixtures.

JIMÉNEZ MAGIC

Raúl Jiménez set a Wolves record by scoring 13 goals in a Premier League season, part of a total of 17 in all competitions – make that 20 if you include his three international goals for Mexico. Jiménez did so well Wolves wasted no time in signing him for £33m when his season long loan from Benfica came to an end. His partnership with Diogo Jota made him simply too hot to handle for Premier League defences as he became Wolves Players' Player of the Season.

THE FIFTIES CLUB

If 40 points is the target to ensure Premier League safety, achieving 50 plus points means a very healthy position in the table. Five clubs were in the 'Fifties Club' last season. Topping those five teams were Wolves with 57 points. They qualified for the Europa League, but what about the other members of the Fifties Club? All of them will be aiming to improve on their points tally and position this time around and all of them are capable of it. Which of these teams do you think has the best chance of pushing into the top six after they occupied seventh to 11th positions last season?

EVERTON

Last Season's Points Total:	54
Last Season's Position:	8th
2018/19 Top Premier League Scorer:	13, Richarlison & Gylfi Sigurdsson
2018/19 Player of the Year:	Lucas Digne

The Toffees' best run of the season came at the end of last year's campaign but they need to find their form sooner this term if they are going to push towards the European places. Only twice did Everton manage back to back victories – their best sequence being a three game winning run in the spring. In contrast back to back defeats were suffered four times. Encouragingly five of their last eight games were victories but the only loss in that run came at doomed Fulham, Everton can't afford slip ups like that.

Test Yourself:
1. Only last season's top three kept more clean sheets than Everton – true or false?

....

LEICESTER CITY

Last Season's Points Total:	52
Last Season's Position:	9th
2018/19 Top Premier League Scorer:	18, Jamie Vardy
2018/19 Player of the Year:	Ricardo Pereira

Having brought instant improvement after taking over in February, former Liverpool boss Brendan Rodgers will be targeting a climb up the table for the 2016 Premier League champions. While West Ham and Watford – who finished just below Leicester – had top scorers with just 10 goals, the Foxes 'fox in the box' Jamie Vardy struck 18 times and is just as likely to get as many again this term. Having a natural scorer is what every team wants and Leicester have one so are a good tip to go higher.

Test Yourself:
2. Were Leicester higher, lower or the same as their eventual 9th place when they sacked manager Claude Puel in February?

....

WEST HAM UNITED

Last Season's Points Total:	52
Last Season's Position:	10th
2018/19 Top Premier League Scorer:	10, Marko Arnautovic
2018/19 Player of the Year:	Lukasz Fabianski

West Ham have the talent to climb higher but do they have the consistency? The fact that their 'keeper was the Irons Player of the Year tells you that they have to work hard to get results. West Ham finished behind Leicester on goal difference – despite scoring one more than the Foxes. Like their fellow Londoners Arsenal, the key to West Ham improving their position rests on them tightening up and being harder to score against. Three of their six clean sheets last season were in big games against Chelsea, Spurs and Arsenal so they can do it – but need to do so more than occasionally.

WATFORD

Last Season's Points Total:	50
Last Season's Position:	11th
2018/19 Top Premier League Scorer:	10, Gerard Deulofeu
2018/19 Player of the Year:	Etienne Capoue

Watford started brilliantly but finished terribly. Even their season highlight turned into disaster when their achievement in reaching the FA Cup final saw them enter the record books by suffering the joint worst final defeat – losing 6-0 to Manchester City. Worryingly, after beating Leicester at the beginning of March, the only points the Hornets took were from a home draw with Southampton and a couple of wins over the teams who ended as the bottom two. The men from Vicarage Road took maximum points from their first 12 games which gave them a head start but can they do as well this season?

Test Yourself:
3. Only the three relegated clubs failed to score in as many matches as West Ham in 2018/19 – true or false?

....

WOLVES

Last Season's Points Total:	57
Last Season's Position:	7th
2018/19 Top Premier League Scorer:	13, Raul Jimenez
2018/19 Player of the Year:	Joao Moutinho

Wolves topped the 'Fifties Club' with a superb season as we saw in our New Gold article!

Test Yourself:
5. Was this Wolves highest finish since 1970, 1980 or 1990?

....

Test Yourself:
4. Last season Watford would have been 7th in the table based on the results of either the first half or second half, but 14th based on the other half. Were they better in the first half or second half?

....

Test yourself answers on page 61

LUCAS DIGNE

Left back – Everton

France international and former Barcelona player, Digne was Everton's Player of the Year and matches quality with consistency.

JORDAN PICKFORD

Goalkeeper – Everton

England's number one. Full of self-belief and still a young goalkeeper who will keep getting better and better. Agile, athletic, brave and brilliant with his distribution.

SHANE DUFFY

Centre back – Brighton & Hove Albion

Resolute in an overworked defence, Duffy still managed to chip in with five goals, being an ever-present danger at set pieces. No one cleared more goals off the line last season than Duffy, who did so four times.

HARRY MAGUIRE

Centre back – Man Utd

Outstanding England defender who was a real stalwart for Leicester. Moved to Manchester United for £80m in the summer.

AARON WAN-BISSAKA

Right back – Man Utd

The Croydon-born right back has been so outstanding he even took Palace's Player of the Year ahead of Wilfried Zaha. All the big clubs showed interest in a player not 22 until a month before Christmas in 2019 and he completed a reported £45m move to Manchester United in the summer.

The PFA Team of the Year was made up of players from Manchester City and Liverpool plus Paul Pogba, but it's not just the top teams who have good players. What do you think of this line up? These players were chosen from teams outside the top seven when the PFA XI was selected, but we think they'd have a pretty strong side!

ASHLEY WESTWOOD

Midfield – Burnley

Quietly efficient playmaker who keeps things simple but effective. Player of the Year at Turf Moor, the former Villa man is the ultimate team player.

CALLUM WILSON

Forward – AFC Bournemouth

14 goals, nine assists and a telepathic understanding with midfielder Fraser. Wilson is a clinical finisher with more than a touch of class.

ÉTIENNE CAPOUE

Midfield – Watford

Physically strong powerhouse who protects his defence but also gets forward. Player of the Year as Watford reached the FA Cup final.

JAMIE VARDY

Forward – Leicester City

With 18 goals and four assists last season with 58% of his shots on target, Jamie Vardy remains one of the Premier League's top scorers. Vardy is a striker defenders never like playing against because he works so hard to put them under pressure.

RYAN FRASER

Midfield – AFC Bournemouth

With 14 assists and seven goals for a club who finished in the bottom half of the table, Fraser is all about end product effectiveness – something every good team needs.

WILFRIED ZAHA

Forward – Crystal Palace

As good as anyone in the Premier League with the ball at his feet, Zaha gets people off their seats with excitement. Previously with Manchester United, many of the big clubs would love to add him to their squads.

PREMIER PUZZLES

SPOT THE DIFFERENCE

Brighton & Hove Albion's Glenn Murray scores his side's first goal against Manchester City in May 2019. Can you spot the six differences?

QUIZ TIME

Give yourself three points for every question you get right. Check the answers on page 61 to see where you rank!

24+	Premier League winner
21+	Champions League place
18+	Europa League place
12+	Mid-table
6+	Avoided relegation
Under 6	Relegated

1) The Premier League's top three scorers in 2018/19 all came from which continent?

2) Which team qualified for the Europa League in their first season after promotion?

3) AFC Bournemouth's Mark Travers became the first teenage goalkeeper to start a Premier League game since 2006. Who was the goalkeeper who did that in 2006 and is now an England international?

4) Which Brazilian scored six times for Everton in his first nine Premier League games for the Toffees?

5) Arsenal have gone three seasons without finishing in the top four of the Premier League. In which season did they last achieve it: 2005, 1995 or 1985?

6) Watford and Brighton lost 0-4 and 0-5 at home to which team in 2018/19?

7) Chelsea's record Premier League defeat came at Manchester City in April. What was the score: 5-0, 6-0 or 7-0?

8) For the first time since 1947/48 a team did not concede a league goal at home to Arsenal, Manchester United, Chelsea or Liverpool. Which club achieved this?

9) Manchester United conceded more goals than in any Premier League campaign. How many: 54, 64 or 74?

10) Who set a Premier League record of going 28 games from the start of the season without a draw?

MANAGERIAL MERRY-GO-ROUND

Each of these managers have managed all of the clubs they are listed with except one — which one?

1) **Mauricio Pochettino**
Aston Villa ☐
Southampton ☐
Spurs ☐

2) **Rafa Benitez**
Liverpool ☐
Southampton ☐
Chelsea ☐

3) **Eddie Howe**
AFC Bournemouth ☐
Burnley ☐
Sheffield United ☐

4) **Sean Dyche**
Burnley ☐
Watford ☐
Brighton ☐

5) **Manuel Pellegrini**
West Ham ☐
Chelsea ☐
Manchester City ☐

Answers on page 61

BEEN THERE BEFORE

The Premier League consists of only 20 clubs but a total of 49 have played in it. Last season Brighton and Hove Albion v Cardiff City became the 100th different fixture to be staged in the Premier League. So, who are the 29 clubs who have been in the Premier League and are dreaming of getting back there one day?

BARNSLEY

The 1997/98 season was the Tykes solitary one in the Premier League.

BLACKPOOL

Under Ian Holloway the Tangerines' only season as members was in 2010/11.

CARDIFF CITY

Relegated last season, the Bluebirds have had two Premier League campaigns.

BIRMINGHAM CITY

The Blues have spent seven seasons in the Premier League, most recently in 2010/11.

BOLTON WANDERERS

Once big hitters under Sam Allardyce, the Trotters dropped out in 2011/12 – unluckily their 13th season in the Premier League.

CHARLTON ATHLETIC

The last of the London club's eight Premier terms was in 2006/07.

COVENTRY CITY

Regulars in the Premier League's early years, the last of the Sky Blues nine seasons was in 2000/01.

BLACKBURN ROVERS

One of only six teams to win the Premier League, the most recent of Rovers' 18 seasons was in 2011/12.

BRADFORD CITY

Now in League Two, the second of the Bantams two Premier League seasons was in 2000/01.

DERBY COUNTY

Losing play-off finalists last season, the Rams came close to an eighth year in the Premier League, having dropped out in 2007/08.

FULHAM

Relegated last season, the Cottagers have spent 14 seasons as Premier League members.

HUDDERSFIELD TOWN

Relegated last season after two seasons at the top level.

HULL CITY

The Tigers have had five seasons as a Premier League outfit, the last in 2016/17.

IPSWICH TOWN

The Tractor Boys have had five years in the Premier League but crashed out in 2001/02.

LEEDS UNITED

Reigning Football League champions when the Premier League began, Leeds have had a total of 12 seasons as Premier League members.

MIDDLESBROUGH

Members of the Premier League in 15 seasons, Boro were relegated in 2016/17.

NOTTINGHAM FOREST

Twice European champions, Forest have spent just five seasons in the Premier League, dropping out in 1998/99.

OLDHAM ATHLETIC

Relegated from the second of their two seasons in 1993/94.

PORTSMOUTH

The south coast club were relegated in 2009/10. They have had seven years in the Premier League.

QPR

Last relegated in 2014/15, the Hoops have had seven seasons in the Premier League.

READING

The last of the Royals' three Premier League campaigns came in 2012/13.

SHEFFIELD WEDNESDAY

The Owls have spent twice as long in the Premier League as their neighbours Sheffield United. This season is the Blades' fourth whilst Wednesday have had eight, but none since 1999/00.

STOKE CITY

Relegated in 2017/18, Stoke have spent 10 seasons in the Premier League.

SUNDERLAND

The most recent of the Black Cats' 16 Premier League seasons was in 2016/17.

SWANSEA CITY

Relegated in 2017/18, the Swans have spent seven seasons in the Premier League.

SWINDON TOWN

The Robins' solitary Premier League season was in 1993/94.

WEST BROMWICH ALBION

The Baggies have had 12 seasons in the Premier League, the most recent being in 2017/18.

WIGAN ATHLETIC

2012/13 was the last of the Latics' eight seasons in the Premier League.

WIMBLEDON

The original Wimbledon had eight Premier League seasons, the last in 1999/00.

FACTS & STATS

Premier League football is full of facts and stats... some more surprising than others! Brush up on your knowledge and prepare to amaze your friends with some of these facts.

In 2018/19 there were 1072 Premier League goals – the most in 20 years.

Scoring the first goal in a game is always important and Manchester City managed this in 34 out of 38 games in 2018/19 – the most ever.

Blackburn Rovers and Leicester City have each won the Premier League once. Manchester United, Chelsea, Arsenal and Manchester City are the other teams to have won the Premier League.

2018/19 saw the lowest number of draws ever in the Premier League – just 71 with Spurs and Man City finishing level just twice each.

34% of games in 2018/19 were won by the away team – the highest ever percentage in the Premier League.

Manchester City led for 2088 minutes and trailed for just 132 minutes in 2018/19.

The first ever Premier League goal was scored by Sheffield United against Manchester United. The scorer was Brian Deane on 15 August 1992.

Fulham lost all 10 London derbies in 2018/19.

The 25,000th goal in the Premier League was scored by Manchester United against Swansea in 2016. The scorer was Zlatan Ibrahimovic.

Between 2004 and 2018 Crystal Palace were awarded more Premier League penalties than either West Ham or Newcastle – despite the Eagles playing over 200 fewer Premier League games in that time than either the Irons or the Magpies.

WINNING PREMIER LEAGUE MANAGERS TABLE

Country	Count	Managers
Italy	4	(Mancini, Ancelotti, Ranieri, Conte)
Scotland	2	(Ferguson, Dalglish)
Chile	1	(Pellegini)
France	1	(Wenger)
Portugal	1	(Mourinho)
Spain	1	(Guardiola)
England	0	

When Chelsea won 6-0 away to Wigan in 2010 the game had no corners.

Derby County only gained 11 points in 2007/08.

In December 1999 Chelsea became the first team to name a starting XI with no players from Britain.

Manchester United beat Ipswich Town 9-0 in 1995.

Andreas Johansson (Wigan 2004), Keith Gillespie (Sheffield United 2007) and Dave Kitson (Reading 2007) all managed to be sent off in Premier League games without touching the ball in the game!

73 years and 57 days – the combined age of Bruno's assist for Glenn Murray's goal for Brighton against Wolves in October 2018 – the Premier League's oldest goal combination!

Richard Dunne scored 10 Premier League own goals.

Sam Allardyce has managed seven clubs in the Premier League. Mark Hughes has managed six (by the start of the 2019/20 season).

Ryan Giggs won 13 Premier League titles with Manchester United.

EAGLES & MAGPIES

CRYSTAL PALACE

Last Season's Points Total:	49
Last Season's Position:	12th
2018/19 Top Premier League Scorer:	12, Luka Milivojevic
2018/19 Player of the Year:	Aaron Wan-Bissaka

Palace were within one win of being part of last season's 'fifties club,' which was a remarkable achievement after a start that saw their only victories from their first 13 games come against two of the sides who went down. A strong finish which saw 26 of their 49 points come from their final 14 games provided exciting times for Palace. If they could maintain that form for a significantly longer spell the Eagles could really take off.

Test Yourself:
1. Ten of top scorer Luka Milivojevic's goals were penalties. Only one man has scored more penalties in a Premier League season and he played for Palace as well. Who was that?

....

NEWCASTLE UNITED

Last Season's Points Total:	45
Last Season's Position:	13th
2018/19 Top Premier League Scorer:	12, Ayoze Perez
2018/19 Player of the Year:	Salomon Rondon

The Magpies finished one place above Bournemouth thanks to a better goal difference. United kept things tight, scoring 14 fewer goals than Bournemouth – but conceding just 48 compared to the Cherries' 70. After 31 games of 2018/19 the Magpies had an identical record to 2017/18 with exactly the same number of wins, draws, losses, goals scored and goals conceded! They ended the season with a point more than the previous season – but finished three places lower.

Test Yourself:
2. Newcastle's only three points from their first 10 games of last season all came from draws with the same score-line, was it 0-0, 1-1 or 2-2?

....

Test yourself answers on page 61

CHERRIES ON TOP

If you like goals watch Bournemouth. There were more goals in Bournemouth's games last season than any other team. In the Cherries 38 Premier League games last season there were 126 goals, 56 for Bournemouth and 70 against. There were 118 in Manchester City's games and 111 in Liverpool's, because those teams score a lot but don't concede many. Only Arsenal came close — with 124 in Gunners' games.

It's easy to think of 'little' AFC Bournemouth when you look at the level of support the Cherries have compared to the teams they take on in the Premier League. While even teams such as Newcastle in the bottom half of the table can command gates of over 50,000, the south coast club have a stadium that holds fewer than 11,500 people.

Until 1987 Bournemouth had never played so high as what is now the Championship and as recently as 2010 they were in League Two, having had a total of 27 points deducted in the previous two seasons. Times were very hard! Since then they have a right to claim to be the most successful club of the decade regardless of, for example, the gigantic achievements of Manchester City. City and the other giants of the game have always been big clubs with vast support and glorious histories.

In Bournemouth's case they won promotion from the bottom tier in 2010, rose from League One three years later and followed that up after another two seasons with promotion to the Premier League in 2015. Since then not only have they stayed there but they have played good football and won plenty of friends along the way.

16th in their first season in the top flight, they did amazingly well to finish in the top half in what is often seen as the difficult second season for promoted clubs. Having been ninth in 2017 the Cherries were 12th two years ago and 14th last term.

Lack of support does not mean lack of ambition or investment. Bournemouth paid big fees for Dominic Solanke and Chris Mepham in January having also paid over £11m for David Brooks at the start of the season — a fee that by the end of the campaign looked a bargain as the former Sheffield United man became a massive hit in the Premier League.

With the dynamic duo of top scorer Callum Wilson and assist king Ryan Fraser (see our Dynamic Duo article for more!) such a devastating combination, Bournemouth are an exciting team to watch — even though they need to tighten up their leaky defence.

Last Season's Points Total:	45
Last Season's Position:	14th
2018/19 Top Premier League Scorer:	14, Callum Wilson
2018/19 Player of the Year:	Ryan Fraser

Test Yourself:
1. Between his two spells as Bournemouth manager which other current Premier League club was managed by Eddie Howe?

....

Test yourself answers on page 61

RISING STARS

There is always room for a new star in the Premier League. Look out for these six stars of tomorrow.

PHIL FODEN
Manchester City – Midfielder

- The youngest player to win a Premier League winner's medal. He now has two but doesn't leave his teens until the end of the season.
- Versatile player who can play anywhere on the left side.
- Has top class vision, reads the game expertly and has the ability to execute the passes he sees.

TOP TALENT – Close control

WESLEY MORAES
Aston Villa – Striker

- Cost Aston Villa a club record £22m in the summer.
- Brazilian who was the best young player in the Belgian league last season.
- Scored 17 goals last term including two in the Champions League.

TOP TALENT– Cool finishing

DWIGHT McNEIL
Burnley – Winger

- Transformed Burnley's fortunes when coming into the Turf Moor team in the second half of last season.
- Claimed three goals and four assists in his 21 games.
- Will make Manchester United regret releasing him.

TOP TALENT – Takes wicked corners

MIGUEL ALMIRON
Newcastle United – Midfielder

- Joined in January so acclimatised to English football before starting his first full season this year.
- Only Mo Salah, Eden Hazard and Raheem Sterling could better all three of Almiron's stats of 19 shots, 12 from inside the box and eight on target in the weeks he played.
- Cost £20m from Atalanta in the MLS.

TOP TALENT – Superfast

CALLUM HUDSON-ODOI
Chelsea – Striker

- Set to play much more often for Chelsea due to the Blues' transfer embargo and the sale of Eden Hazard.
- Already a full England international although still a teenager.
- A World Cup winner at Under 17 level.

TOP TALENT – Skill and power on the ball

FRASER HORNBY
Everton – Striker

- Yet to make a Premier League or domestic cup debut at the start of this season but ready to make his mark.
- Powerful Scotland Under 21 international.
- Playing for a club always ready to give youth a chance.

TOP TALENT – Leads the line with maturity

RECORD BREAKER RASHFORD

George Best, Wayne Rooney and England legend Tommy Lawton are three of the greatest names in the game. Marcus Rashford smashed records set by all of them!

1 His very first club was a boys' side called Fletcher Moss Rangers.

2 Rashford started with United when he was seven.

3 His birthday is on Halloween – which might explain why he is a nightmare for defenders. He was 22 in 2019.

4 In the first game Marcus saw, the Brazilian Ronaldo scored a hat-trick for Real Madrid at Old Trafford in 2003.

5 He scored twice on his first team debut in a Europa League game with Danish club Midtjylland in February 2016, breaking George Best's record as United's youngest ever European scorer.

6 Three months before his debut Rashford was named as a sub in a Premier League game against Watford.

7 He took just three minutes to score on his England debut, against Australia at Sunderland just three months after his United debut.

8 He became England's youngest debutant scorer at 18 years and 209 days, breaking the record set by Tommy Lawton in 1938.

9 Marcus broke Wayne Rooney's record as the youngest player to represent England at a tournament when he played against Wales at Euro 2016 at the age of 18 years and 229 days.

10 He scored on his Champions League debut, against Basle in September 2017.

11 In February 2019 Marcus marked his 100th Premier League appearance with the winner for United at Leicester – a ground he has also scored at for England.

THE NEW BOYS

Norwich City, Sheffield United and Aston Villa have all returned to the Premier League this season. All three are clubs with good support and strong traditions. They will all hope to make the sort of impression Wolves did in their first year after promotion last year. Most of all, they will hope to avoid the immediate relegation which saw Fulham and Cardiff slide straight back into the Championship after promotion a year ago.

A POINT A GAME?

With 38 games, a point from every one of them should keep a side up unless they are very unfortunate. Routinely 40 points is seen as the safety line but no team have been relegated with as many as 38 points since 2011 when Blackpool and Birmingham found that 39 was not enough. Last season 35 points would have been enough to protect a Premier League place, third bottom Cardiff going down on 34 despite a final day win at Manchester United.

FINE FINISHER

If you are going to be a fine finisher you might as well come from Finland. The championship's top scorer, Finland international Teemu Pukki joined the Canaries on a free transfer from Danish club Brondy at the start of the season. Listing Seville, Schalke and Celtic amongst his previous clubs, Pukki took the championship by storm and if Norwich are to do well he needs to keep finding the net regularly against Premier League defences.

CANARIES

Norwich won the Championship by some distance, 11 points clear of third placed Leeds and 18 ahead of Villa who triumphed in the play-offs. Head coach Daniel Farke was under pressure when his side were 17th – a point above the bottom three – after six games but over the next 40 fixtures they took 20 points more than Leeds, who at that time topped the table.

BLADES

Impressive away form in their biggest games was crucial to Sheffield United's promotion. Victory in a crucial show-down at Leeds, who were pushing hard for the second promotion place the Blades achieved, and draws at Norwich and Villa who they went up with, along with a derby stalemate at local rivals Sheffield Wednesday showed how

NORWICH CITY

Last Season's Points Total:	94
Last Season's Position:	1st Championship
2018/19 Top League Scorer:	29, Teemu Pukki
2018/19 Player of the Year:	Teemu Pukki

SHEFFIELD UNITED

Last Season's Points Total:	89
Last Season's Position:	2nd Championship
2018/19 Top League Scorer:	23, Billy Sharp
2018/19 Player of the Year:	David McGoldrick

ASTON VILLA

Last Season's Points Total:	76
Last Season's Position:	5th Championship; Play-off Winners
2018/19 Top League Scorer:	25, Tammy Abraham
2018/19 Player of the Year:	John McGinn

Test Yourself:
1. When Norwich won the Championship in 2019 was it the 1st, 2nd, 3rd or 4th time they had won it, or its equivalent?

Test Yourself:
2. Which two members of England's defence in the 2018 World Cup semi-final used to play for Sheffield United?

Test Yourself:
3. Villa finished in the top six of the Premier League for three years in a row from 2008 to 2010 – true or false?

stubborn United can be. They will need that stubbornness to survive at the top level. The men from the Steel City have the toughness and determination to stay up but whether they have the quality will depend upon who they can bring in, including in the January window.

VILLANS

Villa were two points outside the play-offs when Steve Bruce was sacked after 11 games. Had it not been for Glenn Whelan failing to score with an injury time penalty in Bruce's last match, Villa would have been level with fifth placed Brentford... whose manager Dean Smith replaced Bruce at Villa Park.

Smith invigorated Villa. They went on to break a 109-year old club record for successive wins as he got the best out of talisman Jack Grealish by handing the captaincy to the grandson of Billy Garraty, who won the cup with Villa way back in 1905! Villa came through the play-offs, narrowly beating Frank Lampard's Derby County at Wembley after edging the semi-final over local rivals West Brom on penalties.

Traditionally one of the grandest clubs in the land, former European champions Villa have the power to thrive.

NEVER TOO OLD

Crystal Palace boss Roy Hodgson has become the oldest person to manage in the Premier League.

Turning 72 just as this season started, the former England supremo became the oldest Premier League manager in February when, at the age of 71 years and 192 days, he overtook another ex-England gaffer Sir Bobby Robson as the league's oldest. Former Manchester United manager Sir Alex Ferguson was 71 when he ended his managerial career.

Hodgson has managed The United Arab Emirates, Finland and Switzerland as well as England. He has also managed club sides in six countries including Liverpool and Inter Milan. A league title winner with four of his clubs, the Premier League's elder statesman also took both Fulham and Inter Milan to the final of the UEFA Cup.

As a young player born in Croydon near where Crystal Palace play, Roy Hodgson was a youth team player with the club but left before making a first team debut. He enjoyed a career playing non-league football before becoming a top manager.

Just as many top players fail when they try to become managers, sometimes players who have not had great careers succeed in becoming elite managers. Hodgson started his rise to managerial fame in Sweden, winning the league with Halmstad when he was still in his twenties. Now in his 44th year as a manager, Roy Hodgson has a huge amount of experience and remains as enthusiastic about the game as managers less than half his age.

QUIZ ANSWERS

Pages 28 & 29
Denying the Drop

BRIGHTON: The Premier League trophy – presented to Manchester City

SOUTHAMPTON: Centre forward

BURNLEY: Tom Heaton

Pages 36 & 37
Changing Times

SPURS: Four

ARSENAL: Seven

Pages 38 & 39
Changing Times

MAN CITY: Chelsea

MAN UTD: Cardiff City

Pages 42 & 43
The Fifties Club

EVERTON: True

LEICESTER CITY: Higher

WEST HAM UNITED: True

WATFORD: Second

WOLVES: 1980

Pages 47
Quiz Time

1) Africa
2) Wolves
3) Joe Hart
4) Richarlison
5) 1985
6) AFC Bournemouth
7) 6-0
8) Everton
9) 54
10) Spurs

Managerial Merry-Go-Round

1) Aston Villa
2) Southampton
3) Sheffield United
4) Brighton
5) Chelsea

Page 52
Eagles & Magpies

EAGLES: Andy Johnson

MAGPIES: 0-0

Page 53
Cherries on Top

BOURNEMOUTH: Burnley

Pages 58 & 59
The New Boys

NORWICH: 4th

SHEFFIELD UNITED: Kyle Walker & Harry Maguire

ASTON VILLA: True

Pages 46
Spot the Difference

Crystal Palace's Andros Townsend celebrates scoring his Premier League Goal of the Season against Manchester City at the Etihad Stadium.